SONGHAY

THE KINGDOMS OF AFRICA

SONGHAY

THE EMPIRE BUILDERS

PHILIP KOSLOW

CHELSEA HOUSE PUBLISHERS • New York • Philadelphia

Frontispiece: An engraving of wildlife along the Niger River, from François Gallieni's *Deux campagnes aux Soudan français* (Two Campaigns in the French Sudan, 1891).

On the Cover: An artist's rendering of a Bambara mask; in the background, travelers approach the city of Timbuktu. (Image of mask courtesy of the Buffalo Museum of Science, Buffalo, New York.)

CHELSEA HOUSE PUBLISHERS

Editorial Director Richard Rennert
Executive Managing Editor Karyn Gullen Browne
Copy Chief Robin James
Picture Editor Adrian G. Allen
Art Director Robert Mitchell
Manufacturing Director Gerald Levine
Assistant Art Director Joan Ferrigno

THE KINGDOMS OF AFRICA
Senior Editor Martin Schwabacher

Staff for SONGHAY

Editorial Assistant Sydra Mallery
Designer Cambraia Magalhães
Picture Researcher Wendy Wills
Cover Illustrator Bradford Brown

First Printing
1 3 5 7 9 8 6 4 2

Library of Congress Cataloging-in-Publication Data

Koslow, Philip.
    Songhay: the empire builders / Philip Koslow.
        p. cm.—(The Kingdoms of Africa)
Includes bibliographical references(p.) and index.
    ISBN   0-7910-3128-4
               0-7910-2943-3 (pbk.)

    1. Songhai Empire—Juvenile literature. 2.Songhai (African people)—History—Juvenile litera-
ture. I. Title. II. Series.   94–31095
DT551.45.S66K67 1995   CIP
966.2'018—dc20   AC

CONTENTS

Titles in
THE KINGDOMS OF AFRICA

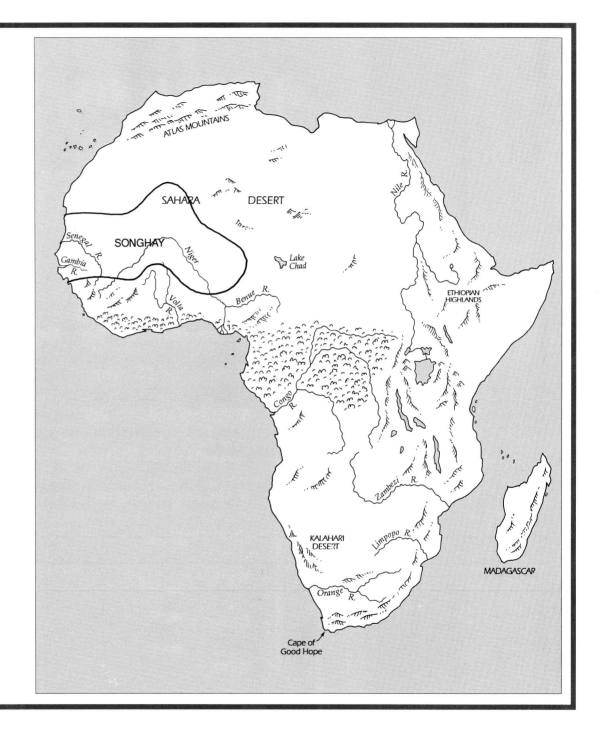

"Civilization and Magnificence"

On a sunny morning in July 1796, Mungo Park, a Scottish doctor turned explorer, achieved a major goal of his long and difficult trek through West Africa when he reached the banks of the mighty Niger River. Along the river was a cluster of four large towns, which together made up the city of Segu, the principal settlement of the Bambara people. The sight of Segu dazzled Park as much as the spectacle of the broad, shining waterway. "The view of this extensive city," he wrote, "the numerous canoes upon the river; the crowded population; and the cultivated state of the surrounding country, formed altogether a prospect of civilization and magnificence, which I little expected to find in the bosom of Africa."

7

Park's account of his journey, *Travels in the Interior Districts of Africa*, became a best-seller in England. But his positive reflections on African civilization were soon brushed aside by the English and other Europeans, who were engaged in a profitable trade in slaves along the West African coast and were eventually to carve up the entire continent into colonies. Later explorers such as Richard Burton, who spoke of the "childishness" and "backwardness" of Africans, achieved more lasting fame than did Park, who drowned during a second expedition to Africa in 1806. Thus it is not surprising that 100 years after Park's arrival at Segu, a professor at England's Oxford University could write with bland self-assurance that African history before the arrival of Europeans had been nothing more than "blank, uninteresting, brutal barbarism." The professor's opinion was published when the British Empire was at its height, and it represented a point of view that was necessary to justify the exploitation of Africans. If, as the professor claimed, Africans had lived in a state of chaos throughout their history, then their

A relief map of Africa, indicating the territory controlled by the Songhay empire.

European conquerors could believe that they were doing a noble deed by imposing their will and their way of life upon Africans.

The view that European colonizers had brought civilization to savages lingered well into the 20th century. But as the century progressed, more enlightened scholars began to take a fresh look at the African past. As archaeologists (scientists who study the physical remains of past societies) explored the sites of former African cities, they found that Africans had enjoyed a high level of civilization hundreds of years before the arrival of Europeans. In many respects, the kingdoms and cities of Africa had been equal to or more advanced than European societies during the same period.

Modern scientists also reject the idea—fostered by Europeans during the time of the slave trade and colonialism—that there is any connection between a people's skin color and their capacity for achievement and self-government. Differences in pigmentation, scientists now recognize, are based solely upon climate and have nothing to do with

8

A view of the village of Kamalia, visited by Mungo Park in 1796. In the engraving, Park is represented as the bearded figure seated under a tree in the right foreground.

intellectual ability. When the human species began to develop in the sun-drenched regions of Africa some 7.5 million years ago, humans were all dark skinned because dark pigmentation protected them from the harmful ultraviolet rays of the sun. However, when humans later migrated from Africa to colder climates where there was far less sunlight, heavy pigmentation became a drawback—it prevented the skin from absorbing the amount of sunlight needed to produce vitamin D, which is essential for the growth of bones and teeth. Hence lighter skin began to predominate in Europe, with the peoples of Asia, the Middle East, and North Africa occupying a middle ground between Europeans and dark-skinned Africans. Rather than indicating superiority, therefore, lighter skin can be viewed as a divergence from the original pigmentation of all human beings.

As early as 400 B.C., a West African people centered in the village of Nok, in present-day Nigeria, produced small sculptures equal in workmanship and beauty to anything created by the widely acclaimed artists of ancient Greece and Rome. By A.D. 750, when most of Europe was still mired in the Dark Ages, the prosperous kingdom of ancient Ghana, known as the Land of Gold, was flourishing in West Africa. When the power of Ghana began to decline during the 12th century, the kings of Mali built an even greater empire and dominated the region during the 13th and 14th centuries. By the 15th century, Mali itself came under attack both from its subjects and neighboring peoples. A new power arose in West Africa, and before long the region witnessed the birth of the greatest empire of all—Songhay.

This sculpture from the ancient city of Jenne in West Africa dates from the 14th century or earlier. The snake depicted on the figure's forehead suggests that the sculpture was used in religious ceremonies; many West Africans regarded snakes as sacred beings.

9

Chapter 1 | REVOLT ALONG THE NIGER

A 19th-century engraving of a Songhay village. Originally farmers in the Sahara region, the Songhay migrated south to the Niger River approximately 4,000 years ago.

One of the most prized possessions of the kingdom of Mali was the city of Gao, located in the middle Niger, just below the point at which the mighty river makes its great bend to the south. Known to the Arab traders as Kaw-Kaw, Gao was the arrival point for the trading caravans that made their way across the Sahara Desert to West Africa from the wealthy land of Egypt. Gao was also well located to receive caravans coming from the eastern regions of North Africa. At Gao, the traders could either refresh themselves before moving on or else ship their merchandise along the Niger to other trading centers in the Sudan. (West Africa as a whole was known to the Arabs as *Bilad al-Sudan*, "the Land of the Black Peoples.")

When the kings of Mali conquered Gao during the 13th century, the city already had a rich history dating back hundreds of years. Gao had been established at the beginning of the 7th century by the Songhay people. The Songhay (pronounced SAUN-ghi) consisted of two principal clans: the Sorko, who fished along the Niger, and the Gabibi, who were farmers. The Songhay differed in several ways from the Soninke and the Malinke, who had founded the empires of Ghana and Mali, respectively. Whereas the Soninke and Malinke spoke languages belonging to the Mande family, West Africa's dominant language group, the Songhay language belonged to the Nilo-Saharan family. Thus, the Songhay language shared a common root with the

12

languages of peoples who lived to the north and the east of the Sudan, especially the Berbers of the Sahara. This connection had been established thousands of years earlier, when the Songhay had also inhabited the Sahara, at that time a green and fertile area that provided a home for many peoples who raised crops and livestock. The drying-out of the Sahara, which was completed by about 2000 B.C., caused the Songhay to move south and finally created a barrier between the peoples of the North and those of the interior. But trade between the two regions never ceased entirely: North Africans continued to visit the interior by means of horse-drawn chariots. When the camel was introduced to North Africa during the 4th century A.D., making the journey across the Sahara somewhat easier, the Songhay were in an excellent position to reap the benefits of increased trade.

By the 10th century, the Songhay had built a substantial state along the Niger. The state was ruled by kings who bore the title *dia* and who probably belonged to a group that had intermarried with the Berbers. At this time the dias resided in Kukya, a city to the south of Gao along the Niger. Early in the 11th century, the capital of the Songhay shifted to Gao, following a pivotal event that took place in 1010: the conversion of Dia Kossoi to the religion of Islam.

Islam had arisen in the deserts of Arabia, to the east of Africa. The inhabitants of Arabia, who were mainly farmers and wandering herders, had for centuries worshiped a variety of gods and spirits, many of them associated with forces of nature. In this form of worship, the Arabians were following the traditions of the earliest inhabitants of the Middle East, peoples such as the Sumerians and Assyrians, who had created the world's first great civilizations. As they honored these age-old beliefs, however, the Arabians were in close contact with peoples who practiced more recent religions, such as Judaism and Christianity, which were based upon worship of a single god. Both religions had been founded by powerful figures who had experienced what they believed to be a direct communication from God, revealing a great truth for all humanity.

The prophet who emerged to express a new religious idea in Arabia was named Muhammad. Born in the city of Mecca in 570, Muhammad spent his youth as a camel driver and then became a tradesman. At the age of 40, he had a vision of a new religion based on the worship of a

Muslim warriors in battle, as depicted in a 14th-century Persian manuscript. After the death of Muhammad in 632, his followers swept through Arabia, North Africa, and Spain, spreading the Muslim faith.

13

single god, Allah, who demanded strict devotion, regular prayer, and pure habits in return for eternal salvation. Muhammad quickly attracted a group of followers, but he also aroused bitter opposition among the Arabian tribespeople, who felt that he was attacking their traditional beliefs and way of life. In 622, Muhammad's enemies forced him to leave Mecca and resettle in Medina. There he continued to gather converts, who became known as Muslims, and to develop the principles that grew into the religion of Islam. By the time of Muhammad's death in 632, his powerful influence had spread throughout Arabia. His teaching was recorded in the holy book known as the Koran, which has the same importance for Muslims as the Old Testament has for Jews and the New Testament has for Christians.

The Great Mosque of Kairouan, in the North African nation of Tunisia, dates from the 7th century A.D. and was built shortly after the Muslim conquest of North Africa. As a result of the influence of North African traders, the Songhay king Kossoi converted to Islam in 1010.

Muhammad's followers, led by the prophet's father-in-law Abu Bakr, set out to spread their faith and culture. By 645, Muslim warriors had conquered all of Arabia and much of the Middle East. From there they moved westward into the central part of North Africa, known as the Maghrib. By the end of the 7th century, the Muslims had extended their power to the Atlantic coast of Africa, and shortly afterward they crossed the Strait of Gibraltar to conquer much of present-day Spain and Portugal.

Despite their zeal for conquest, the Muslims were known for their general tolerance in religious matters. They made no attempt to convert Christians and Jews, whom they considered "peoples of the Book," and they converted those they considered "pagans" only when there was a political advantage in doing so. For this reason, the Muslims did not attempt to extend their rule to West Africa; the undertaking would have been too difficult, and they had more to gain from maintaining friendly relations with their trading partners.

Though they were not forced to become Muslims, West African rulers and traders found that adopting Islam offered political and economic advantages. The moral codes of the Islamic faith were closely related to business practices—Muhammad himself had been a merchant. In the long-distance trade across the Sahara, a shared sense of values was important to insure security and credit. Islam offered this bond of trust between different ethnic groups.

Viewed in this light, the conversion of Dia Kossoi was a natural result of the trans-Sahara trade. Like other West African rulers before him, Dia Kossoi was eager to make the Muslim traders feel at home in his realm, and sharing their religion was the most direct way of gaining their confidence. In one respect, this strategy was too successful for the Songhays' own good. By the 13th century, Gao's increasing wealth made the city an attractive prize for the Muslim kings of Mali, who already controlled the trading centers of Jenne and Timbuktu on the western branch of the Niger. It is likely that Mali's armies conquered Gao somewhere between 1285 and 1300. The Malians did not find it easy to dominate the city; when Mansa Musa, one of Mali's greatest rulers, passed through Gao on the way back from his spectacular 1324–25 pilgrimage to Mecca, he took the opportunity to build a mosque in the city and reassert his rule. By the following century, however, the kings of Mali were no longer strong enough to control Gao, and the Songhay rose under the leadership of the Sunni dynasty.

Sekene Cissoko, a historian from the West African nation of Senegal, has described the course of events leading to Songhay's independence: "The Sunni, also known as Sii or Shi, were warriors. The last three of the line [of Sunni kings] left Gao and carried the war westwards towards the . . . empire of Mali. Sunni Madawu . . . embarked on a great raiding expedition against Niani, the capital of the Mandingo empire, and sacked it, carrying off 24 slave tribes belonging to the mansa. His successor, Sunni Sulayman Daama, in his turn invaded and destroyed Nema . . . and carried off considerable booty. The wars increased the monarch's scope for action. The king of Gao became the real master of the Niger Bend." At this stage in Songhay history, the time was ripe for the emergence of a true empire builder.

15

Chapter 2 | SUNNI ALI THE GREAT

A mounted figure sculpted by the Dogon people of Mali. During the early history of West Africa, the horse was a major factor in the building of kingdoms and empires: the skillful use of cavalry forces enabled such powerful rulers as Songhay's Sunni Ali to conquer vast territories.

Sunni Ali became king of the Songhay in 1464 and quickly established himself as a peerless military leader. According to the *Tarikh al-Fattash* (The History of the Seeker of Knowledge), a lengthy chronicle begun during the 16th century by a black West African Muslim, Sunni Ali was "always victorious and sacked every country on which he had designs. Not one of his armies, as long as he was at its head, was ever routed: he was always the conqueror, never the conquered. Between Kanta and Sibiridugu [from the Niger valley to the north of modern-day Dahomey], there was not a single region, a single city, a single village that he did not attack at the head of his cavalry, waging war against the inhabitants and ravaging their territory."

In swift succession, Sunni Ali defeated the Mossi, the Dogon, and the Fulani, all formidable neighbors who had been raiding the territory surrounding Songhay. According to the *Tarikh al-Fattash*, Sunni Ali showed no mercy to these peoples: "There was no enemy he hated more than the Peuls [Fulani], and he could not set eyes on a Peul without killing that person, whether learned or ignorant, man or woman. . . . He decimated the tribe of the Sangare until nothing remained of them but a tiny fraction, which could be gathered in the shade of a single tree."

Having secured Songhay's frontiers, Sunni Ali took the offensive. In 1468, he captured Timbuktu, which had been taken by the Tuaregs 35 years earlier. Then he turned his attention to Jenne, the richest of all the trading centers along the Niger. Jenne was situated in the flood plain of the Niger, and the seasonal rising of the waters provided the city with a priceless natural defense against invaders. Tradition had it that Jenne had withstood 99 separate attacks by the kings of Mali, but still the determined Sunni Ali began a siege of the city.

Siege warfare was a common procedure during the Middle Ages. Unable to take a fortified city by head-on assault, the attacker would simply surround it and cut off its food supplies, until the defenders were starved into submission. Remarkably, Jenne held out for seven years. Each time the Niger rose, Sunni Ali's forces were obliged to pull back, but still they persevered. By 1476, both the attackers and the defenders of Jenne were on the verge of starvation, and even the invincible Sunni Ali was becoming discouraged. Just as he was about to lift the siege, however, Jenne surrendered. Sunni Ali thus added another rich prize to his domain.

In dealing with the residents of the conquered city, Sunni Ali showed restraint and mercy. This was not surprising, because many Muslims lived in Jenne, and Sunni Ali had followed his predecessors in adopting the religion of Islam. However, the fate of Timbuktu, also a Muslim city, had been far different. There, the Muslim leaders had aroused Sunni Ali's wrath, in part because they had cooperated with the Tuareg while the latter controlled the city. Even

18

Depicting a figure in a posture of submission, this sculpture from Mali expresses the fate of the peoples subdued by Sunni Ali. Between 1468 and 1476, the Songhay ruler overran the lands of the former empire of Mali, capturing the rich trading cities of Timbuktu and Jenne.

though some of the same leaders later helped Sunni Ali take the city, he decided to stamp them out. Those who escaped Sunni Ali's executioners by fleeing north to Walata found that they were still not out of danger. Sunni Ali was so eager to get his hands on them that he conceived a fantastic project. He proposed to dig a 200-mile-long canal from the Niger to Walata so that he could employ his naval forces against the city. Reportedly, he was only diverted from this scheme by the threat of renewed attacks by the Mossi.

Sunni Ali's punishment of the Muslims of Timbuktu was so severe that even after his death the residents of the city regarded his memory with awestruck horror. The author of the *Tarikh al-Fattash* referred to him as "the tyrant, the debauched, the accursed, the oppressor" and accused him of the most hideous cruelties: "Sunni Ali was a tyrannical king, so heartless that he would sometimes throw an infant into a mortar and force its mother to grind it to death with a pestle. . . . The remains would then be fed to the horses." Though the lurid details of the story may well be exaggerated, they indicate the lasting impact of Sunni Ali's persecutions on the minds of Timbuktu's people.

This wooden war helmet was carved by an artist in the present-day nation of Burkina Faso, formerly part of the Songhay empire. According to a West African chronicle, "There was not a single region, a single city, a single village that [Sunni Ali] did not attack at the head of his cavalry."

19

Beyond his desire for revenge, Sunni Ali's treatment of the Muslims in Timbuktu also had a political purpose. He was wise enough to recognize that his greatest support came from the original

20

A sculpture of a ram's head from Mali. The ram plays an important role in many West African religions, which honor the spirits of nature. Although Islam made many converts in the cities of Songhay, most of the country people continued to follow their age-old beliefs.

Songhay cities, Gao and Kukya, and from the Songhay farmers and fishermen, who had ignored Islam in favor of their traditional beliefs. The conflict between cultures was especially severe in the case of Timbuktu, where many of the citizenry made a particular issue of their connection to the North Africans. As E. W. Bovill has written in *The Golden Trade of the Moors*, "The people of Timbuktu had black skins, but much Berber blood flowed in their veins, and so proud were they of it that they scorned the negroid Songhai as uncouth savages, although their ruling house was of Berber origin." This attitude undoubtedly irked Sunni Ali from a personal point of view. Perhaps more important, when he ravaged Timbuktu he was showing the Songhay people that he would not tolerate insults to their honor.

Sunni Ali did follow the royal tradition by adopting Islam, but there is no indication that he devoutly observed Muslim rites. While paying his respects to the religion of the North African traders, he was careful to present himself to his own people as one who upheld the ancient Songhay beliefs. Traditional religion centered on the forces of nature, represented by various spirits and by sacred animals such as the snake and the ram. In particular, the Songhay worshiped Harke Dikko, the god of the Niger, and Dongo, the thunder god. They also paid homage to the spirits of their ancestors and employed magic healers, known as *soni-anke,* to protect them from evil forces and sorcerers. Like their counterparts in many other cultures, Songhay farmers and fishermen believed that they could only prosper by living in harmony with nature. Many of their rituals were designed to gain favor with the spirits of the natural world, ensuring that the soil would bear abundant crops and the rivers would teem with fish. The concept of a single, all-powerful god who presided over the world from a heavenly abode was foreign to the Songhay's thinking and way of life.

Even where they made converts, Muslim holy men did not demand too much in the way of piety. They interfered as little as possible with the age-old beliefs of the Sudanese and in many cases tried to make Islam more appealing by adapting it to local needs and customs. For example, they were known to provide West Africans with written prayers from the Koran that could be used as amulets, or charms. When wrapped in a piece of snakeskin, the tip of a sheep's horn, or some other item that could be fastened about the neck or ankle, these prayers were believed to protect the wearer from injury or bad luck. When Mungo Park visited the Sudan at the end of the 18th century, he observed that these amulets were still highly prized.

As long as Sunni Ali continued his spectacular string of military conquests, there was little danger that any outside forces would threaten the harmony of this cultural balance. Commanding loyalty, respect, fear, and obedience, he created an empire that far surpassed both ancient Ghana and Mali. But after his death in 1492, it became immediately clear that the strength of this empire depended greatly upon the personality of its leader.

21

Chapter 3 | ASKIA MUHAMMAD

A page from the Koran, Islam's holy book, reproduced in a Moroccan manuscript. Many kings of Songhay adopted Islam purely for political reasons; but Askia Muhammad, who took the throne in 1493, was a devout Muslim remembered for his many acts of piety.

In 1492, Sunni Baru inherited the crown of his illustrious father, Sunni Ali. Though he assumed great power and vast wealth, he could not recapture his father's aura of success. Before he had spent a year on the throne, he was faced with a serious rebellion. The root of the problem was Sunni Baru's refusal to adopt Islam, even on the most superficial level. In taking this course of action, he clearly believed that he was reinforcing the base of his power among the Songhay. But he soon found that he had underestimated the danger of taking sides so openly.

The Muslims of the towns had submitted to Sunni Ali because he had known how to blend force and diplomacy. While making them fear the consequences of displeasing him, he also persuaded the Muslims that he appreciated their contribution to the prosperity of the Songhay empire. Sunni Baru's open hostility convinced the Muslims that they were about to lose their influence in the royal court. They may have also believed that Sunni Baru was a far less dangerous enemy than his father had been. Concluding that they now had little to lose by rebelling against the king, they rallied behind Muhammad Turay, a high-ranking army official. Only 14 months into Sunni Baru's reign, Muhammad Turay defeated him in battle and replaced him on the throne.

Muhammad Turay, who became known as Askia Muhammad, ruled Songhay from 1493 to 1528. By taking the title *askia*, a military rank in the Songhay army, rather than the traditional royal title *sunni*, he announced his desire to break with the past. Indeed, the reign of Askia Muhammad brought about a dramatic shift in power from the countryside to the cities—not at all suprising, considering that the new ruler's main support had come from the Muslims of the towns.

Askia Muhammad was careful not to alienate Songhay's traditional villagers, thus avoiding the error Sunni Baru had made in turning his back on a large segment of the nation's population. Nevertheless, Askia Muhammad's actions made it plain that his adherence to Islam was more than a mere political gesture. As a result, the author of the *Tarikh al-Fattash* described him in terms of admiration far different from the abuse heaped upon Sunni Ali: "He had a lively affection for the *ulama* [the community of Muslim scholars and teachers]. . . . He was extremely generous with alms and performed many acts of devotion that went beyond the prescribed religious duties."

Among the acts of charity ascribed to Askia Muhammad in the *Tarikh al-Fattash*, one in particular shows that he was acutely aware of his need to restore goodwill for the monarchy among the Muslims of Songhay: "In the course of the year [1507–8] he made his camp at Kabara, where he met three descendants of Sheik Haugaro. . . . They complained vigorously to Askia Muhammad about the cruelties and ill treatment they had endured in the days of Sunni Ali; the askia gave them compensation in the form of 10 slaves and 100 cows, and they departed for their homes."

The outstanding proof of Askia Muhammad's devotion to Islam was his pilgrimage in 1496–97 to Mecca, the birthplace of the Prophet. On his journey, Askia Muhammad was accompanied by 500 mounted warriors and 1,000 foot soldiers, and he carried with him 300,000 *dinars*—more than a ton of gold coins—to cover his expenses. No West African king had made such a spectacular display of wealth and power since 1324, when Mansa Musa, the ruler of Mali, had undertaken his own pilgrimage to the holy places of Islam.

The religion of Islam requires its followers to make the pilgrimage, or hajj, at least once in a lifetime, if they have the means to do so. According to the historian Albert Hourani, more than 50,000 pilgrims—most of them from Egypt and the Middle East—traveled to Mecca each year during the 15th century. Hourani has described the typical observances followed by these devotees:

(Continued on page 29)

24

A TRAVELER ON THE NIGER

Heinrich Barth, a German scholar and linguist, visited the heart of the former Songhay empire during the early 1850s, making detailed observations on the landscape and the people. The illustrations that follow are taken from his book *Travels and Discoveries in North and Central Africa.*

A view of Kabara, the harbor of Timbuktu. "During the palmy days of the Songhay empire," Barth wrote, "a numerous fleet was always lying here under the orders of an admiral of great power and influence."

The camp of Sheikh Ahmed el-Bakay, on the outskirts of Timbuktu. El-Bakay assured Barth's safety in the region by writing a letter addressed to other Muslim chiefs, in which he declared, "Lo! I love my guest the Christian. Be careful that he is not hindered in anything."

An encampment of Tuareg herders at Amallele, a stream branching off the Niger. In the background, cattle graze in one of the swampy meadows that form in the Niger Delta after the rainy season.

A view of Foga, a village in the northeastern reaches of the former Songhay empire. According to Barth, the residents of Foga obtained salt by filtering water through mounds of soil and then boiling the water until only the natural minerals remained.

(Continued from page 24)

At a certain point on the approach to Mecca, the pilgrim would purify himself by ablutions [ritual baths], put on a white garment made of a single cloth, the *ihram*, and proclaim his intention to make the pilgrimage. . . . Once he arrived in Mecca, the pilgrim would enter the sacred area, the *haram*, where were various sites and buildings with hallowed associations. . . . At the heart of the *haram* stood the *Ka'ba*, the rectangular building which Muhammad had purged of idols and made the center of Muslim devotion, with the Black Stone imbedded in one of its walls. The pilgrims

A view of Mecca, to which Askia Muhammad made a pilgrimage in 1496–97. In the foreground is the Ka'ba, a massive stone structure that is the holiest shrine of Islam. The first duty of a pilgrim to Mecca is to circle the Ka'ba seven times, a devotion known as the tawaf.

30

The tomb of Askia Muhammad, located near the city of Gao. During Askia Muhammad's reign (1493–1528), Songhay became the greatest empire in the history of West Africa.

would go round the Ka'ba seven times, touching or kissing the Black Stone as they passed it. On the eighth day of the month they would go out of the city in the eastern direction to the hill of 'Arafa. There they would stand for a time, and this was the essential part of the pilgrimage. On the way back to Mecca, at Mina, two more symbolic acts would be performed: the casting of stones at a pillar signifying the Devil, and the sacrifice of an animal. This marked the end of the period of dedication which had begun with the putting on of the *ihram*; the pilgrim would take off the garment and return to the ways of ordinary life.

In the view of the *Tarikh al-Fattash,* Askia Muhammad's journey was a complete success, both spiritually and politically: "The inhabitants of the two noble cities [Mecca and Medina] turned out to greet him; in the glorious city of Mecca,

he bought a plot of land on which he built a house, and he set the house up according to the plan of the noble temple of Ka'ba; there he had interviews with illustrious doctors of the faith and other pious and reverend individuals. The sharif of Mecca [a descendant of Muhammad] bestowed the investiture of Muslim sovereignty upon him by placing a blue turban on his head and awarding him the title of *imam* [Muslim leader]."

Like Mansa Musa before him, Askia Muhammad returned home with an even greater sense of his royal power, a deepened religious faith, and a new appreciation of the refined culture of the Muslim world. He was determined to maintain his realm in a style equal to that of the nations he had visited, and in pursuing this goal he would achieve a level of greatness unmatched by any previous West African ruler.

31

Chapter 4 | THE GLORY OF SONGHAY

A 19th-century engraving of a West African market. The wealth of Songhay depended in large part on the great caravans—some of them containing as many as 12,000 camels—that plied the trade routes across the Sahara.

Though remembered most for his piety and political genius, Askia Muhammad was also an outstanding military leader in the tradition of Sunni Ali. During his reign he conducted campaigns that greatly increased the territory of Songhay. At its greatest extent, the Songhay empire encompassed all the lands formerly controlled by the empires of ancient Ghana and Mali, including the gold-producing regions of Bambuk and Bure. Songhay also pushed eastward, as Askia Muhammad exacted tribute from Kano and Zaria, two of the leading Hausa city-states. The askia's realm eventually reached north into the fringes of the Sahara, bringing the valuable salt mines of Teghaza under the control of Songhay. Thus Songhay became the greatest empire in the history of West Africa.

The management of far-flung territories had always posed a challenge to West Africans, who had long been used to living in smaller communities that were based on kinship and ruled by chiefs or elders. With the rise of ancient Ghana during the 10th century, centralized government took hold in the Sudan. Rulers such as Tunka Manin of Ghana and Mansa Musa of Mali divided their realms into provinces that were governed by local chiefs or governors, all of whom paid taxes to the king and pledged their support in time of war. In the case of Mali, the king also appointed royal officials to perform important governmental functions. Because the wealth of both em-

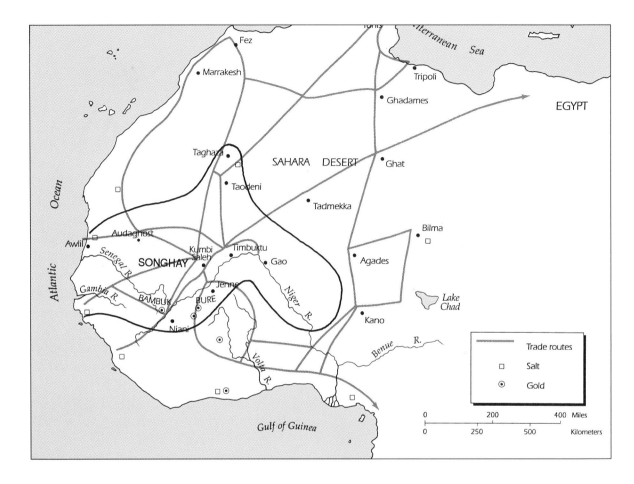

A map of Songhay during the 16th century, when the askias extended their power to the salt mines of Teghaza in the North and Hausaland in the East.

pires depended upon trade, it was especially important for the kings to maintain order throughout the realm and provide security for traders' caravans.

Finding himself in command of more territory than any previous West African ruler, Askia Muhammad was inspired to develop the art of government to a new level of sophistication. Sunni Ali had made a number of innovations in this area; the great conqueror had created new provinces, improved farming methods, and organized the Sorko boatmen of the Niger into the beginnings of a profes-

34

sional navy. Askia Muhammad built upon these foundations and went far beyond his predecessor's achievements.

One of Askia Muhammad's greatest innovations was to open up the ranks of government service. While honoring the tradition of appointing governors and other officials on the basis of birth, he also applied the Muslim principle of equality, which valued learning and piety more than ancestry. Under Askia Muhammad's reign, able individuals could achieve high office regardless of their social standing. With this innovation, Askia Muhammad created a system of government that anticipated the modern concept of a professional civil service.

The empire of Songhay was divided into five provinces: Kurmina, Dendi, Baro, Dirma, and Bangu. Each province was governed by an official who used the title *fari* or *farin*. Kurmina ranked as the most important province, and thus the *kurmina fari* was the highest-ranking official of Songhay. This post was always held by the king's brother, who was designated to succeed him on the throne. The first kurmina fari, Askia Muhammad's brother Umar Komdiago, even established his own capital at Tendirma. Here he maintained his own court, independent of the royal court at Gao.

The emperor's court at Gao was a scene of splendor: when the ruler appeared in public to address the concerns of the people, he followed the West African custom of sitting on a raised platform covered by festive silk umbrellas, and he was always surrounded by hundreds of servants and lesser officials. The king was also splendidly attired: according to the *Tarikh al-Fattash*, his wardrobe contained more than 200 sets of silk, woolen, and cotton clothing—much of it imported from the great cloth centers of Europe. Following another time-honored Sudanese practice, the king never spoke directly with any of his subjects. All communications were addressed to the king's *griot*, or herald, a figure who was both an official spokesman and a historian who preserved and recited accounts of the king's exploits. When the king replied to requests from his subjects, he spoke softly to the griot, who then repeated the king's remarks in a loud voice.

The central government was elaborately organized, employing a host of royal officials who bore the titles *farma* and *koi*. Unlike previous rulers, Askia Muhammad was not content to have a single official in charge of each important governmental function. He also appointed a host of subofficials, creating a

35

36

structure much like the system of ministers, secretaries, and undersecretaries of modern nations. For example, Songhay's *katisi farma* (finance minister) was assisted by the *waney farma*, who handled all questions of property; the *bara farma*, who looked after the payment of wages; and the *dey farma*, who was in charge of all purchasing done by the government. These officials had heavy responsibilities. As Sekene Cissoko has pointed out, the rulers of Songhay both collected and spent large sums of goods and money: "There were the revenues from the sovereign's personal property, the *zakat* or tithe collected for the poor, taxes in kind levied on harvests, herds and fishing, taxes and customs duties on commercial activity, special levies on the merchants of large towns and, above all, the spoils of almost annual war. . . . A large proportion of [the sovereign's] income went to the upkeep of the court and the standing army. The askia also contributed to the construction or restoration of the mosques, supported the poor of his empire, and gave presents and alms to the great marabouts [Muslim holy men]."

Other important officials included the *fari mondzo* (minister of agriculture), the *hari farma* (commissioner of waters and lakes), and the *korei farma*, who was in charge of relations with foreigners. Most governmental decisions were made by a royal council composed of Songhay's leading officials.

Askia Muhammad took great pains to modernize his military forces, building on the work of Sunni Ali. Previously, West African rulers had recruited armies in time of war and disbanded them when the need was over, often relying on subject princes to provide manpower. In this way, the kings were spared the expense of maintaining a standing army. During the 15th and 16th centuries, when methods of warfare were becoming more sophisticated, training and discipline were all the more important. A body of amateur soldiers who had been taken from peacetime pursuits could hardly perform as well as a corps of professionals who had the benefit of constant training.

According to Sekene Cissoko, the Songhay military forces consisted of approximately 100,000 infantry and 10,000 cavalry: "Armed with long lances, sabres and arrows, the Songhay mounted warriors wore iron breastplates beneath their battle tunics. . . . The infantry were armed with spears and arrows and carried leather or copper shields. The Niger fishermen. . . made up a permanent flotilla of nearly 2,000 dugout canoes on the

Canoes along the Niger River. Among the achievements of Songhay's rulers was the creation of a professional navy made up of Niger boatmen. The boats themselves were rarely armed, but in time of war they provided swift transport for masses of troops.

river. The army carried long trumpets (*kakaki*) and standards and had their own marching order and fan-shaped battle formation." The commanding general of the army bore the title *dyini koi*; the *hi koi* was the chief admiral of the navy; a third official, the *tara farma*, was in charge of the cavalry.

Summing up the brilliant innovations of Askia Muhammad, E. W. Bovill has written, "His people were less indebted to him for the vast empire he gave them, than for his teaching them organized government by which alone could security and prosperity be achieved." In the case of Songhay, good government resulted not only in wealth and power but also in a flowering of culture that surpassed anything that the Sudan had previously experienced.

Chapter 5 | TRADERS AND SCHOLARS

For many years, historians believed that the ancient cities of West Africa owed their existence to Muslim traders, who brought their rich culture, nurtured in the great metropolitan centers of Egypt and North Africa, into the agricultural world of the Sudan. More recently, however, researchers have uncovered clear evidence that Jenne, in particular, was a thriving city well before the extension of trade to the Niger region during the 9th and 10th centuries. Known as Jenne-Jeno, the original settlement dates back to the 3rd century B.C.

The Great Mosque of Jenne, built in the 14th century, is still in use today. Built on an island in the Bani River, a tributary of the Niger, Jenne has been a flourishing community since the 3rd century B.C.

Long before the coming of the Muslims, the black African residents of Jenne-Jeno were growing rice and other crops and working various metals, including iron. They had already begun their own trading network with other re-

gions of the continent. According to the Senegalese scholar Djibril Niane, "Jenne was a major importer of copper, which it exchanged in the south for gold, kola nuts, and ivory. The discovery of copper at Jenne and Igbo-Ukwu [in the Niger delta] dating from before the eighth century prove that the Arabs were responsible only for a wider extension of trans-Saharan trade. The commercial activities of the Wangara or Dioula [Mandingo peoples renowned as traders] preceded the coming of the Arabs; war and trade allowed them to expand their influence greatly in all directions."

Niane believes that the present-day city of Jenne supplanted Jenne-Jeno when the growing number of Muslim residents felt the need to establish an Islamic community separate from the

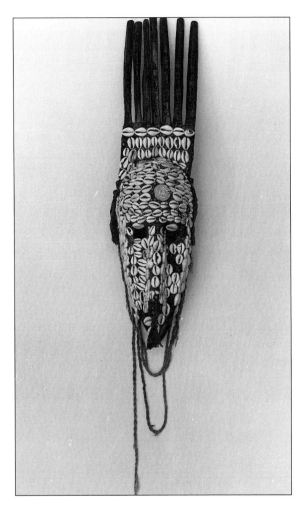

This West African mask is decorated with cowrie shells, the major form of currency used by the residents of Songhay. During the 16th century, 500 cowries were equal to one-eighth of an ounce of gold.

40

original inhabitants, who practiced traditional religions. A public prayer recited by the city's Muslim community, as recorded in the *Tarikh al-Fattash*, indicates that commerce also played a crucial role in the life of the growing city: "Let everyone who emigrated out of his own country out of distress and poverty be given by Allah wealth and prosperity, so that he will forget his home country; let the foreigners in the town be more numerous than its local people; let patience be taken away from those who come to the town for trade, that they . . . will sell their merchandise to its people cheap, so that the latter make great profits."

Until the invincible Sunni Ali took the city, Jenne had been protected from invaders for more than 800 years by its location in the flood plain of the Niger. Jenne was thus able to develop into the most secure and prosperous community in the Sudan. Gao and Timbuktu may have been more important depots for the great caravans—each one typically consisting of several thousand camels—that entered West Africa from the Sahara. But Jenne was the crucial link between the foreign traders and the all-important gold mines of the southern forest belt.

Emerging from the Sahara after a perilous two-month journey, the caravans carried salt, copper, glassware, and textiles. Salt has always been an especially precious commodity in the scorching climate of the Sudan, where essential minerals are quickly lost through perspi-

A rooftop view of Timbuktu, from a 19th-century engraving. Songhay's most populous city, Timbuktu was noted for its intellectual culture, which produced the first works of literature by black Africans.

ration. At Timbuktu, rectangular slabs of salt were unloaded from the traders' camels and shipped along the Niger to Jenne by canoe. At Jenne, the salt was broken into smaller pieces, which could then be carried south into the forest belt by donkeys or porters. In exchange for the salt and other goods, the forest dwellers would provide gold dust mined at Bambuk and Bure; ivory obtained from the teeth of hippopotamuses and the tusks of elephants; and kola nuts, which were valued as a stimulant and thirst quencher (the original formula for Coca-Cola contained an ingredient derived from kola nuts). Areas of the south that were not rich in gold, ivory, or kolas often paid for imported goods with slaves who had been captured in warfare.

In everyday transactions, only the Muslim traders used gold dust or gold coins. The Sudanese purchased their necessities with chunks of salt, pieces of iron, or cowrie shells. The cowries were the most common form of currency in West Africa. The small white shells were harvested in the Indian Ocean and imported to the Sudan in quantities that were carefully regulated by the authorities in order to maintain their value. During the 16th century, the rate of exchange between cowrie shells and gold was one *mitqal* (one-eighth of an ounce of gold) to 500 cowries.

At the height of Songhay's power, Jenne's total population stood between 30,000 and 40,000; Timbuktu was inhabited by about 80,000 people and Gao by as many as 100,000. Sekene Cissoko has described the rich and varied cultures that blended in the three main cities:

> All these towns of the Niger had a dominant Songhay nucleus, whose language was widely spoken. But they also had a cosmopolitan population of Berber Arabs, Mossi, Hausa, Mandingo (Wangara), Soninke, Fulani and others. . . . Urban society contained three basic elements: the merchants, the craftsmen and the religious orders, all gaining a living directly or indirectly from commerce.

Of the three great towns, Timbuktu had the most tumultuous history, having been raided so often by the Tuareg. (Even Sunni Ali could never subdue the Tuareg, who repeatedly took refuge in the vast Sahara desert, where no pursuing army could survive.) Perhaps for this reason, the city also possessed the most vibrant and sophisticated society. Leo Africanus, a Muslim traveler who visited Songhay during the reign of Askia Muhammad, described Timbuktu in enthu-

42

siastic terms: "The inhabitants are people of a gentle and cheerful disposition, and spend a great part of the night in singing and dancing through all the streets of the city. Here are great store of doctors, judges, priests and other learned men, that are bountifully maintained at the king's cost and charges. And hither are brought diverse manuscripts of written books out of Barbary [North Africa], which are sold for more than any other merchandise."

43

A 19th-century engraving of a Muslim school in Jenne. As the rulers of Songhay brought scholars and teachers from all parts of the Muslim world into their realm, the cities of the Niger became major centers of Islamic learning.

44

The art of literature reached new heights under Askia Muhammad and his successors. Traditionally, few West Africans knew how to read and write. Living close to the land and depending for their survival on an expert knowledge of the natural world, they had concentrated on practical arts such as farming, fishing, mining, hunting, and weaving. They expressed their spiritual and artistic impulses by creating sculptures that rank among the great masterpieces of world art. The Africans' practical wisdom was often bound up with religious beliefs, which they did not wish to expose to unworthy persons. (The Dogon people of Mali, for example, have created an elaborate religious and philosophical system whose doctrines are understood only by a handful of holy men.) Instead of keeping written records, therefore, West Africans relied upon oral traditions that were passed on from one generation to the next, usually by the griots. These traditions survive to the present day, and scholars have found them remarkably accurate in their portrayal of past events.

As the great empires of the Sudan developed and their forms of government became increasingly complicated, oral communication proved to be inadequate. In a small state, rulers could easily convey their orders to officials by word of mouth. In a large empire, where messengers had to travel long distances, verbal commands were highly unreliable as compared to written instructions. For this reason, rulers had been using Muslims to keep written records in Arabic since the days of ancient Ghana. The kings of Mali in particular had sent their subjects to study in such Islamic centers as Fez and Cairo and had encouraged Muslim teachers to set up schools in the Sudan. With the rise of Songhay, Timbuktu itself became a major center of learning. "In the sixteenth century," Sekene Cissoko has written, "Timbuktu had some 180 Koranic schools and thousands of students from every corner of the Sudan and the Sahel, who lived with their teachers as lodgers. . . . The Sudanese university . . . taught the humanities, which included the traditional academic subjects—theology (tawhid), exegesis (tafsir), traditions (hadith), and Malikite [orthodox Muslim] jurisprudence—as well as grammar, rhetoric, logic, astrology, astronomy, history and geography."

During the 16th and 17th centuries, this system produced a number of important native-born writers. The most prominent was Mahmoud Kati, the author of the Tarikh al-Fattash. Born in Timbuktu

(Continued on page 49)

ARTISTS OF THE SUDAN

At its height, the Songhay empire extended its sway over many other West African peoples, including the Mandingo, Mossi, Fulani, Dogon, and Bambara. Though all these groups paid tribute to the Songhay rulers, they always maintained their distinctive languages, beliefs, and arts. During the 400 years since the decline of Songhay, the Sudan's diverse cultures have continued to flourish, producing some of the world's most remarkable artworks.

Fragment of a statuette in the "multiple eyelid" style, sculpted in Jenne during the 15th century. The artists of ancient Jenne, predominantly Mandingo, were organized into occupational castes, like shoemakers, blacksmiths, and musicians; thus, the children of sculptors would be expected to follow their parents' profession.

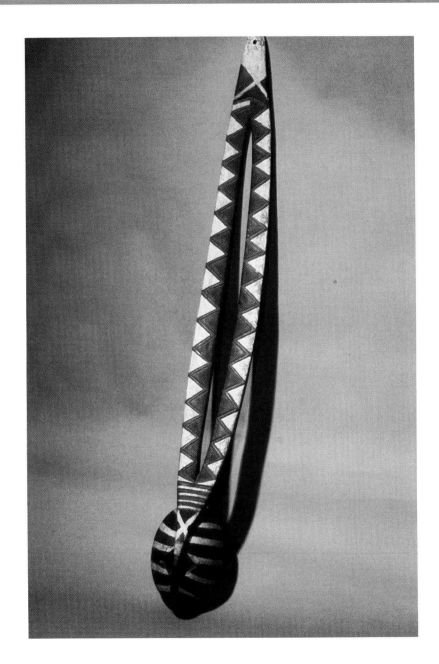

Mossi antelope mask. In his book The Arts of Black Africa, *the art historian Jean Laude has explained the importance of masks in various African ceremonies: "A mask is a being that protects the wearer. It is designed to absorb the life-force that escapes from a human being or from an animal at the moment of death."*

A terra-cotta Bambara vessel dating from the 19th century. In a number of West African societies, the wives of blacksmiths have practiced the art of pottery.

A wooden sculpture of a nummo, created by the Dogon people of present-day Mali. In the complex religious philosophy of the Dogon, the nummo are the guiding spirits involved in the creation of the world.

(Continued from page 44)

around 1468, Kati became a member of Askia Muhammad's staff and accompanied the king on his great pilgrimage to Mecca in 1496. Uniquely qualified to record the events of the times, he began his great work in 1518 and continued it throughout his life, which reportedly lasted 125 years. After Kati's death, his sons continued working on the *Tarikh*, bringing it to completion in 1665.

Abd al-Rahman as-Sadi, who lived between 1596 and 1655, wrote the second of Songhay's great histories, the *Tarikh as-Sudan* (History of the Sudan), which includes valuable accounts of ancient Ghana and Mali as well as Songhay. A third writer from Timbuktu, Ahmad Baba, compiled a vast private library and wrote a number of works on Islamic law that are still used by Muslim scholars in West Africa. When the French explorer René Caillié visited Timbuktu and Jenne in 1828, he was impressed to observe that all the inhabitants were able to read and write in Arabic.

Adding the luster of scholarship to its wealth and power, Songhay should have been equal to any challenge that confronted it. But neither wealth nor culture could protect Songhay against the greed and lust for power that have afflicted all the great empires in history.

For all his piety, energy, and vision, even Askia Muhammad could not, in the end, control his own destiny or the fate of the empire he had built. E. W. Bovill has described the last chapter of the askia's life and the beginning of Songhay's undoing: "Three of his sons, led by the eldest, Musa, rebelled against him. Now an old man and worn out in the service of his country, he summoned his brother Yahia to his aid. But the sons killed Yahia, marched into Gao and forced Askia to abdicate in favor of Musa. Thus ended in 1528 the reign of perhaps the greatest monarch that ever ruled in the Western Sudan."

Chapter 6 | THE FATE OF SONGHAY

A 16th-century West African sculpture of a Portuguese soldier wielding a harquebus, an early type of musket. When Moroccan forces defeated the Songhay armies at the Battle of Tondibi in 1591, the victory was due in large part to the Moroccans' use of harquebuses.

After Askia Muhammad's ouster, his sons vied with one another for control of the empire, often engaging in bloody struggles for supremacy. Musa ruled for only three years; Muhammad II Benkan Kirai lasted for seven; Ismail reigned a mere two years. Stability finally returned under Askia Dawud, the youngest of Askia Muhammad's sons, who reigned from 1549 to 1583. Indeed, some historians believe that Songhay achieved its highest degree of power and prosperity under Askia Dawud, who had accumulated a great deal of experience in government during his father's reign and had been wise enough to learn from his brothers' mistakes.

After the death of Askia Dawud, his own sons resumed the example of their uncles by battling one another for the throne. During the short reign of Askia Muhammad III (1583–86), the Hausa states in the East stopped paying tribute to Songhay, and the Moroccans of North Africa seized control of the valuable salt mines at Teghaza. The Moroccans had been claiming ownership of the mines since the 1540s, and their territorial ambitions soon led to a full-scale war between Morocco and Songhay.

The Moroccans were formidable warriors. In 1578, they had successfully defended their territory against an invading force from the European nation of Portugal, annihilating the Portuguese king Dom Sebastian and 25,000 of his soldiers at the Battle of the Three Kings. By this victory, they delayed the European

52

penetration of Africa by more than two centuries.

In 1591, Morocco's sultan Mulay Ahmad al-Mansur, known as Mulay the Victorious, sent an army of about 4,000 men south through the Sahara to plunder the riches of Songhay. Such a small force should not have stood much chance against the powerful armies of Songhay, but the invaders had several important factors weighing in their favor. First, at least half of them were equipped with harquebuses. The harquebus, a European invention, was an early form of firearm that provided a tremendous advantage over opponents armed only with swords, lances, and bows and arrows. Second, many of the Moroccan troops were Spanish and Portuguese Christians who had been taken prisoner in war or captured by Muslim pirates in the Mediterranean Sea. Their lives had been spared on the condition that they convert to Islam and fight for the sultan. Though they had no personal loyalty to Mulay, they knew that retreat would mean either a slow death in the Sahara or execution when they returned to Morocco—thus, they fought with the ferocity of desperate men. Finally, Songhay itself was struggling to recover from a civil war that had pitted the western provinces against Gao:

the central government had prevailed under Askia Ishak II, but many of the defeated westerners were openly supporting the Moroccans.

The first battle between Morocco and Songhay, which took place at Tondibi on March 12, 1591, resulted in a clear-cut victory for the invaders. Fighting their way steadily southward, they penetrated both Gao and Timbuktu and carried off much gold and other goods. The weakened armies of Ishak II proved unable to drive the Moroccans back across the desert, but the country people did what they could to harass the invaders. In his *Tarikh as-Sudan*, Abd al-Rahman as-Sadi provided a vivid account of the chaos and destruction caused by Mulay's troops: "This expeditionary force found the Sudan one of God's most favored countries in prosperity, comfort, security, and vitality. . . . Then all that changed; security gave place to danger, prosperity made way for misery and calamity, whilst affliction and distress succeeded well being. Over the length and breadth of the land people began to devour one another, raids and war spared neither life nor wealth. Disorder spread and intensified until it became universal."

The Moroccans never succeeded in pacifying all the former territories of

Songhay. They contented themselves with setting up garrisons in a number of important cities and encouraged immigration from North Africa in the hope of establishing a strong North African colony in the Sudan. The colony was administered from Timbuktu by an official known as a pasha. On the whole, the country people were left to their own devices and followed their traditional religions under the guidance of local chiefs, who often carved out their own spheres of influence by force of arms.

The rule of the pashas proved to be remarkably durable, lasting through the 17th and 18th centuries. The last pasha served until 1826, when Timbuktu fell to the Fulani, Sunni Ali's old enemies, who had also conquered Jenne seven years earlier. Two years later, when René Caillié made his way to Timbuktu in the guise of a Muslim, he found the city reduced to a population of about 12,000. This was a direct result of the natural disasters that had afflicted the Sudan during the previous 100 years, as recurring droughts wiped out crops and a series of deadly plagues ravaged the population. Caillié learned that Timbuktu was now subject to constant harassment by the Tuareg, who raided and plundered without fear of reprisal. Twenty years later, another

European traveler, Heinrich Barth, also observed that the legendary city was less dazzling than he had hoped. But Barth noted that Timbuktu was still the center of a prosperous trade, as the heavily laden camels continued to enter the city from the Sahara and Hausaland.

By this time, the entire political structure of West Africa had been disrupted by the presence of European slave traders, who had been transporting tens of thousands of Africans to the Americas. By the end of the 19th century, the Europeans—particularly the French, Belgians, Germans, and British—had agreed to carve up Africa into colonies.

The Niger area was targeted for domination by France. Whereas the British

A group of Tuareg herdsmen with their flocks. One of the few peoples able to survive in the harsh conditions of the Sahara Desert, the fierce Tuareg raided Timbuktu at will after the power of Songhay crumbled.

53

often tried to gain their objectives in Africa by signing trade agreements, the French relied almost exclusively on military force. Writing of the period between 1880 and 1914, the Senegalese historian M. Gueye points out that "never in the known history of the continent has so much military action been seen and so many invasions and campaigns launched against African states and communities." By 1894, French forces overcame the determined resistance of the Fulani and the Mandingo and took control of Timbuktu.

During the colonial period, the French broke up the former territory of Songhay and formed a huge colony known as the French Sudan, which they strove to develop into a major source of agricultural products. Following World War II (1939–45), African nationalism became an irrepressible force, and in 1960, France's West African possessions achieved their independence, under such outstanding leaders as Léopold Senghor and Sékou Touré. Under the new national boundaries, the territory that had once been the Songhay empire was divided between the nations of Mali, Niger, Nigeria, Senegal, Mauretania, and Upper Volta. The cities of Timbuktu, Jenne, Gao, and Kukya now lie within the borders of the Republic of Mali; the former eastern territories of the empire are situated in the Niger Republic and Nigeria. The cities' ancient mosques are still in use, and in Jenne the Monday market is an especially colorful and vibrant scene, enlivened by the presence of splendidly dressed Fulani women wearing elaborate gold and silver jewelry.

A map of present-day Africa. The shaded area indicates the territory once controlled by Songhay.

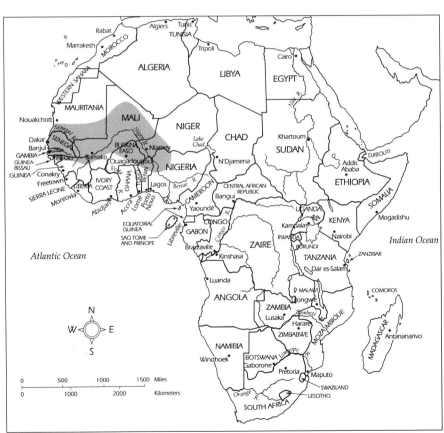

54

In Mali and Niger, nearly a million Songhay still live along the Niger River, fishing and farming as their ancestors did. Many still perform traditional Songhay ceremonies to influence the spirits who govern the river and bring much-needed rain for the crops. The Songhay past remains vibrantly alive in these ceremonies and in the words of the griots. In *Fusion of the Worlds*, a study of Songhay life during the 1980s, Paul Stoller observes that the griots "generally recite their praise-poetry at formal ceremonies: births, weddings, homecomings, initiations of chiefs, and other political festivals. . . . The bard's recitation of the name of a person's celebrated ancestor is believed to imbue that person with the force of that ancestor."

The Songhay's traditional music performs the same function. When musicians play the drum known as the *gasi*, the varying rhythms recall the drumbeats that inspired the troops of Sunni Ali and Askia Muhammad as they went into battle. The gasi is often accompanied by the *godji*, a one-string violin that produces a high-pitched, wailing tone. As Stoller has written, "The godji is at least as old as the Songhay people. . . . Adamu Jenitongo told me that 'the sound of the godji penetrates us and makes us feel the

A solitary fisherman casts his net along the Niger. The Sorko fishing clans still play a major role in the culture of the Songhay people, who consider the Sorko to be valuable companions when traveling on the river. It is believed that they communicate with the spirits of the Niger and that any vessel that carries a Sorko will be free from harm.

presence of the ancestors. . . . We hear the sound and know that we are on the path of the ancestors.' " By maintaining their way of life in the face of many environmental and political challenges, the Songhay demonstrate the qualities that created one of the world's great empires.

55

CHRONOLOGY

10th century	Songhay people create a large state along the Niger River
1010	Songhay ruler Dia Kossoi adopts the religion of Islam, solidifying relations between Songhay and North Africa
11th century	The Songhay move their capital from Kukya to the major trading city of Gao
c. 1300	Kings of Mali conquer Gao
early 15th century	Led by the Sunni dynasty, the Songhay recapture Gao, invade the territory of Mali, and take control of the Niger bend
1464	Sunni Ali becomes king of Songhay
1468	Sunni Ali conquers Timbuktu and punishes the city's Muslim leaders
1476	Sunni Ali captures Jenne, following a seven-year siege
1492	Death of Sunni Ali; Sunni Baru inherits the throne but is deposed after only 14 months
1493	Askia Muhammad becomes ruler of Songhay; during his rule the empire reaches its highest level of development
1496–97	Askia Muhammad makes pilgrimage to Mecca

1518	Mahmoud Kati begins *Tarikh al-Fattash* (History of the Seeker of Knowledge), a written chronicle of the Songhay empire
1528	Askia Muhammad is deposed by his sons; dies one year later
1528–49	Songhay enters a period of turmoil as Askia Muhammad's sons vie for power
1549–83	Reign of Askia Dawud; Songhay enjoys a period of renewed prosperity and stability
1591	Moroccan invaders defeat Songhay's armies at the Battle of Tondibi; Songhay empire begins to dissolve

FURTHER READING

Africanus, Leo. *History and Description of Africa.* 3 vols. Reprint of the 1661 edition. New York: Hakluyt Society/Burt Franklin, n.d.

Ajayi, J. F. Ade, and M. Crowder, eds. *History of West Africa.* 2 vols. London: Longman, 1974.

as-Sadi, Abd al-Rahman. *Tarikh as-Sudan.* French translation by O. Houdas. Paris: Adrien-Maisonneuve, 1964.

Bovill, E. W. *The Golden Trade of the Moors.* Oxford: Oxford University Press, 1968.

Connah, Graham. *African Civilizations.* Cambridge: Cambridge University Press, 1987.

Davidson, Basil. *Africa in History.* Rev. ed. New York: Collier, 1991.

———. *The African Genius.* Boston: Little, Brown, 1969.

———. *The Lost Cities of Africa.* Rev. ed. Boston: Little, Brown, 1987.

Davidson, Basil, with F. K. Buah and the advice of J. F. A. Ajayi. *A History of West Africa, 1000–1800.* Rev. ed. London: Longman, 1977.

Gillon, Werner. *A Short History of African Art.* New York: Penguin, 1986.

Grove, A. T. *The Changing Geography of Africa.* 2nd ed. Oxford: Oxford University Press, 1993.

Hibbert, Christopher. *Africa Explored.* New York: Viking Penguin, 1982.

Hourani, Albert. *A History of the Arab Peoples.* New York: Warner Books, 1992.

Hull, Richard W. *African Cities and Towns Before the European Conquest.* New York: Norton, 1976.

Kati, Mahmoud. *Tarikh al-Fattash.* French translation by O. Houdas and M. Delafosse. Paris: Adrien-Maisonneuve, 1964.

Koslow, Philip. *Centuries of Greatness: The West African Kingdoms, 750–1900.* New York: Chelsea House, 1994.

Kwamena-Poh, Michael, et al. *African History in Maps.* London: Longman, 1982.

Park, Mungo. *Travels in the Interior Districts of Africa.* Reprint of the 1799 edition. New York: Arno Press/New York Times, 1971.

Stoller, Paul. *Fusion of the Worlds.* Chicago: University of Chicago Press, 1989.

Trimingham, John S. *A History of Islam in West Africa.* London: University of Oxford Press, 1962.

———. *Islam in West Africa.* Oxford: Clarendon Press, 1959.

UNESCO General History of Africa. 7 vols. Berkeley: University of California Press, 1980-92.

Webster, J. B., and A. A. Boahen, with M. Tidy. *The Revolutionary Years: West Africa Since 1800.* New ed. London: Longman, 1980.

GLOSSARY

archaeology	the study of the physical remains of past human societies
askia	title used by the later kings of Songhay
clan	a group in African society united by descent from a common ancestor; also known as a descent line
colonialism	domination and economic exploitation of a land and its people by a foreign power
conversion	the act of renouncing one religion and adopting another
cowrie	a small white shell that is harvested in the Indian Ocean, used as currency by many West Africans
dia	title used by the early kings of Songhay
dinar	basic monetary unit of the Muslim world, equal to one-eighth of an ounce of gold, or one *mitqal*
fari (farin)	title used by the governors of Songhay's provinces
farma	title used by high government officials in Songhay
griot	an African storyteller who preserves the oral traditions of a people

Islam	the religion based upon worship of Allah and acceptance of Muhammad as his prophet
koi	title used by high government officials in Songhay
Koran	the holy book of Islam
mosque	a Muslim house of worship
Muslim	one who follows the religion of Islam
oral tradition	a form of historical record in which events are passed on through generations of storytellers instead of being written down
pilgrimage	a journey made for religious purposes
Songhay (SAUN-ghi)	African people speaking a language of the Nilo-Saharan family and inhabiting the region near the Niger bend in present-day Mali; founders of the Songhay empire
Sudan	the region of sub-Saharan Africa stretching from the Atlantic coast to the valley of the Nile River; derives from *Bilad al-Sudan,* Arabic for "Land of the Black Peoples"
sunni	title used by rulers of Songhay during the 15th century
Tuareg (TWAR-egg)	North African Muslims who live as herders in the Sahara and often raided the territory of Songhay

INDEX

PHILIP KOSLOW earned his B.A. and M.A. degrees from New York University and went on to teach and conduct research at Oxford University, where his interest in medieval European and African history was awakened. The editor of numerous volumes for young adults, he is also the author of *El Cid* in Chelsea House's HISPANICS OF ACHIEVEMENT series and *Centuries of Greatness: The West African Kingdoms, 750–1900* in the Chelsea House MILESTONES IN BLACK AMERICAN HISTORY series.

PICTURE CREDITS